Word Study Notebook

Donald R. Bear • Marcia Invernizzi • Francine Johnston

Contents

continued next page

CELEBRATION PRESS
Pearson Learning Group

The following people have contributed to the development of this product:

Art and Design: Sherri Hieber-Day, Dorothea Fox, Jane Heelan, David Mager, Judy Mahoney, Elbaliz Mendez, Dan Thomas
Editorial: Leslie Feierstone-Barna, Linda Dorf, Linette Mathewson, Tracey Randinelli
Inventory: Yvette Higgins
Marketing: Christine Fleming
Production/Manufacturing: Alan Dalgleish
Publishing Operations: Jennifer Van Der Heide

All photography © Pearson Education, Inc. (PEI) unless otherwise specifically noted.

Cover: *l.* © Harvey Lloyd/Corbis Stock Market. **Interior:** *beach* © Klaus Lahnstein/Stone/Getty Images, Inc.; *beak* © Harvey Lloyd/Corbis Stock Market; *bed* © Brownie Harris/Corbis; *bride* © Naideau/Corbis Stock Market; *bridge* Susan Van Etten/PhotoEdit; *chick* Tim Davis/Stone; *crab* R. Calvert/Stone; *deer* Superstock; *dive* David Madison/Stone; *dream* © Philip Coblentz/Digital Vision/Getty Images, Inc.; *drill* © Andy Crawford/DK Images; *duck* S. Nielsen/Imagery; *fish* Carmela Leszczynski/Animals Animals; *fox* Darrell Gulin/Stone; *goat* © James Marshall/Corbis Stock Market; *hill* Superstock; *horse* Robert Maier/Animals Animals; *ice cream cone* © C Squared Studios/Photodisc/Getty Images, Inc.; *moth* © Photodisc/Jim Wehtje/Getty Images, Inc.; *mule* Robert Maier/Animals Animals; *pig* © Don Mason/Corbis Stock Market; *ram* Thomas Kitchin/Tom Stack & Associates; *road* Bill Bachmann/PhotoEdit; *sheep* Ralph A. Reinhold/Animals Animals; *ship* Superstock; *skunk* D. Robert Franz/Stone/Getty Images, Inc.; *sky* John Lemker/Earth Scenes; *smoke* Francis Lepine/Earth Scenes; *snake* Superstock; *stair* Peter Gridley/FPG International; *train* Walter C. Lankenau/Evergreen Graphics; *tree* Jack Wilburn/Earth Scenes; *tune* Dorey A. Sparre/Parker/Boon Productions for Pearson Learning; *twins* © Ken Kaminesky/Corbis; *web* J.C. Stevenson/Animals Animals; *whale* Fred Felleman/Stone; *wheat* Kevin Morris/Stone; *worm* Oxford Scientific Films/Animals Animals.

COVER ART: Zoe Argiriou, age 6; Shane Brockway, age 7; Sehta Fe, age 7.

Celebration Press® is a registered trademark of Addison-Wesley Educational Publishers, Inc. Words Their Way™ is a trademark of Pearson Education, Inc.

ISBN 0-7652-6760-8

Printed in the United States of America

18 19 20 21 V064 14 13 12 11 10

Celebration Press
Pearson Learning Group

1-800-321-3106
www.pearsonlearning.com

Sort 1: Initial Consonant Blends br, sm, tr, sk, dr With Long and Short Vowels

3

dr			

sk			

tr			

sm			

br			

Sort 1: Initial Consonant Blends br, sm, tr, sk, dr With Long and Short Vowels

Draw a picture of something that begins with br, sm, tr, sk, and dr. Write the word below each picture.

br	sm →	tr

sk	dr

Consonant Digraphs ch, sh, wh, th

Sort 2: Consonant Digraphs ch, sh, wh, th With Long and Short Vowels

7

Consonant Digraphs ch, sh, wh, th

th	wh	sh	ch

Sort 2: Consonant Digraphs ch, sh, wh, th With Long and Short Vowels

ch 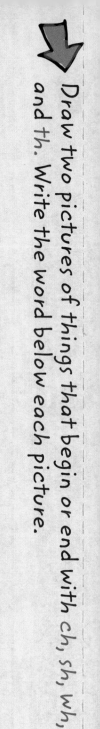	sh	wh	th

| frame | bag | snake | rain |
| train | crane | crab | ram |

| map | bat | jack | skate |
| train | crane | crab | ram |

ā rake

ă cat

Draw two pictures of things with short a and long a. Write the word below each picture.

ă cat	ā rake

Sort 3: Short and Long Vowel a

slide	smile	chin	zip
hill	dive	bike	pig
kite	twins	crib	write

ī vine

ǐ fish

Draw two pictures of things with short i and long i.
Write the word below each picture.

ĭ fish	ī vine

Sort 4: Short and Long Vowel i

nose	log	sock	toe
bone	goat	top	frog
coat	clock	fox	hose

ō globe

ŏ mop

Draw two pictures of things with short o and long o.
Write the word below each picture.

ŏ mop

ō globe

Sort 5: Short and Long Vowel o

juice	fruit	run	thumb
drum	cube	tube	truck
duck	glue	tune	rug

ū mule

ŭ cup

Draw two pictures of things with short u and long u.
Write the word below each picture.

ŭ cup	ū mule

Sort 6: Short and Long Vowel u

pen	feet	jeans	tree
desk	web	nest	beads
dream	sled	ten	leaf

ē sleep

ĕ bed

Draw two pictures of things with short e and long e.
Write the word below each picture.

ĕ [bed image] bed	ē [sleep image] sleep

Review Long Vowels a, e, i, o, u

| cube | cape | cheese | tube | beak |
| rope | dive | bike | tape | cone |

ū	ō	ī	ē	ā
mule	globe	vine	sleep	rake

Say each long vowel word. Write on the lines words from the box that show each long vowel sound.

beak	tube	cheese	cape	cube
float	tape	bike	dive	rope

ā rake

ē sleep

ī vine

ō globe

ū mule

pack	smoke	look
crook	sock	lick
truck	hook	woke
like	book	bake
lock	duck	cook
brook	rake	bike

-ck short	-ke long	-k other
kick	take	took

kick

take

took

Sort 9: Final /k/ Sound Spelled -ck, -ke, or -k

brain	dash	frame
faint	camp	train
stamp	blame	paint
said	snake	crane
snack	want	main
flash	place	snail
bake	black	

Short a (CVC) and Long a (CVCe and CVVC)

ă CVC	ā CVCe	ā CVVC	Oddball
cat	face	rain	

Say each short a and long a word. Write on the lines words from the box that have each vowel sound.

brain	frame	camp	train	dash	faint
snake	snail	paint	crane	place	blame
flash	black	main	snack	bake	stamp

ă cat	ā face	ā rain

Sort 10: Short a (CVC) and Long a (CVCe and CVVC)

clock	note	stone
none	crop	chose
whole	cross	slope
boat	joke	float
coat	love	shop
lock	toast	soap
knock	toad	

ŏ CVC	ō CVCe	ō CVVC	
lost	drove	road	

Say each short o and long o word. Write on the lines words from the box that have each vowel sound.

clock	stone	soap	slope	cross	note
float	whole	crop	toad	chose	toast
shop	lock	joke	knock	coat	boat

Ŏ lost

Ō road

Ō drove

Sort 11: Short o (CVC) and Long o (CVCe and CVVC)

prune	cute	bloom
bump	flute	skunk
tooth	build	trust
grunt	bruise	smooth
built	plus	juice
crude	spoon	mule
suit	cruise	moon

ŭ CVC	ū CVCe	ūi CVVC	ōō CVVC	
crust	cube	fruit	food	

Say each short u and long u word. Write on the lines words from the box that have each vowel sound.

mule	bloom	cute	cruise
flute	skunk	tooth	trust
suit	grunt	juice	moon

ŭ crust

ū cube

ūi fruit

ōo food

keep	sweep	vest
next	jeep	team
leaf	when	teeth
sleep	week	heat
west	wheat	been
clean	web	weak
dress		

Short e (CVC) and Long e (CVVC)

ĕ CVC	ēe CVVC	ēa CVVC	
less	feet	mean	

Say each short e and long e word. Write on the lines words from the box that have each vowel sound.

sweep	vest	team	clean	web	heat
next	teeth	west	sleep	keep	dress
when	wheat	jeep	leaf	weak	week

ĕ less	ēe feet	ēa mean

reach	street	head
queen	great	steam
bread	sweet	bead
dream	thread	best
beach	desk	greed
web	breath	sleep
next	sled	threat

More Short e (CVC and CVVC) and Long e (CVVC)

	ĕ CVC	ĕa CVVC	ēe CVVC	ēa CVVC	
	when	dead	trees	each	

Say each short e and long e word. Write on the lines words from the box that have each vowel sound.

head	queen	best	bead
desk	dream	street	bread
sleep	reach	next	threat

ĕ when

_____

_____

_____

ĕa dead

_____

_____

_____

ēe trees

_____

_____

_____

ēa each

_____

_____

_____

wait	beet	beast	throat
pail	need	cream	beach
train	sheep	coat	coast
wheel	grain	goat	seat
toast	tail	three	neat
road	cheat	cheek	bait

ea	ee	oa	ai

ai	oa	ee	ea

Short a (CVC) and Long a
(CVCe, CVVC-ai, and Open Syllable-ay)

past	taste	drain	blame
raise	shape	stand	shade
stray	brain	grain	smash
stay	wade	play	clay
gain	trash	brave	grass
nail	class	tray	gray

Short a (CVC) and Long a (CVCe, CVVC-ai, and Open Syllable-ay)

ă CVC	ā CVCe	āi CVVC	āy CVV
glass	trade	Spain	lay

Sort 16: Short a (CVC) and Long a (CVCe, CVVC-ai, and Open Syllable-ay)

ă CVC	ā CVCe	āi CVVC	āy CVV
glass	trade	Spain	lay

play	blame	drain
shade	stand	clay
smash	grain	brain
		past
		shape
		stray

Short o (CVC) and Long o (CVCe, CVVC-oa, and Open Syllable-ow)

drop	wrote	roam	slow	long
shop	globe	boat	roast	blow
note	throw	know	gloss	loaf
close	chop	grow	lose	dome
				coach

ŏ CVC	ō CVCe	ōa CVVC	ōw CVV	
stock	froze	coal	show	

Say each short o and long o word. Write on the lines words from the box that have each vowel sound.

coach	drop	dome	shop
blow	roast	throw	chop
loaf	grow	wrote	globe

ŏ CVC **stock**	ō CVCe **froze**	ōa CVVC **coal**	ōw CVV **show**

Sort 17: Short o (CVC) and Long o (CVCe, CVVC-oa, and Open Syllable-ow)

plump	clue	brush
stew	true	knew
sue	blue	glue
sew	do	grew
few	dump	truth
trunk	drew	truck
chew	flue	junk

ŭ CVC	ēw CVV	ūe CVV	
thumb	new	due	

Say each short u and long u word. Write on the lines words from the box that have each vowel sound.

plump	clue	brush	stew	true	knew
flue	chew	sue	blue	glue	grew
few	dump	trunk	drew	truck	junk

ŭ CVC	ēw CVV	ūe CVV
thumb	**new**	**due**

sigh	bliss	night
try	twice	quit
bright	white	dry
fight	cry	whisk
grill	grim	quite
high	shy	rise
grime	sky	

Short i (CVC) and Long i (CVCe, VCC-igh, and CV Open Syllable-y)

ĭ CVC	ī i CVCe	ī igh VCC	ȳ=ī CV
quick	write	might	why

Sort 19: Short i (CVC) and Long i (CVCe, VCC-igh, and CV Open Syllable-y)   (77)

Say each short i and long i word. Write on the lines words from the box that have each vowel pattern.

dry	sigh	bliss	night	try	fight	quite	quit
bright	white	cry	whisk	grime	sky	grill	twice

ĭ CVC	ī CVCe	īgh VCC	y=ī CV
quick	write	might	why

both	find	fond
wish	roll	kiss
lost	slick	blind
will	cold	mind
gold	mild	scold
child	moss	kind
most	pond	fist

Short i, o (CVVC) and Long i, o (VCC)

ĭ CVCC	ī VCC	ŏ CVCC	ō VCC
film	wild	loss	told

Say each short and long vowel word. Write on the lines words from the box that have each vowel sound and pattern.

pond	most	roll	kiss	lost	blind	will	find
cold	child	mild	wish	both	moss	fist	fond

ĭ CVCC	ī VCC	ŏ CVCC	ō VCC
film	wild	loss	told

Sort
21

crew	school	way	soak
shone	bleed	grave	glow
drew	light	slave	grind
ghost	sold	crow	glide
fold	bride	jail	blind
scene	fly	steep	sneak

CV & CVV Open Syllable	CVCe	CVVC	CVCC

Say each long vowel word. Write on the lines words from the box that have each vowel sound and pattern.

grave	light	soak	school	steep	grind	way	fold
scene	glow	sold	jail	glide	crew	shone	drew

CVCC	CVVC	CVCe	CV & CVV Open Syllable

86 Sort 21: Review Long Vowel Patterns

r-Influenced Vowel Patterns ar, are, air

dark	bear	stair	fare
heart	chair	square	start
harm	bare	lair	sharp
pear	fair	pair	stare
wear	hare	shark	where

ar	are	air	Oddball
part	care	hair	

Say each word aloud. Write on the line a word that sounds the same but is spelled differently and has a different meaning. Then draw a picture of the word you wrote.

pair	stare	bare
————	————	————

fare	where	hare
————	————	————

Sort 22: r-Influenced Vowel Patterns ar, are, air

earth	deer	ear	perch
clerk	spear	fern	steer
jeer	learn	herd	fear
heard	dear	germ	rear
			peer

er	ear	eer	Oddball
her	clear	cheer	

Write on the lines words with the same vowel sound and pattern as her, clear, and cheer.

her	clear	cheer

r-Influenced Vowel Patterns ir, ire, ier

third	flier	purse	hire
wire	clerk	girl	tire
crier	birth	fur	shirt
first	her	sire	pliers
			umpire

ir	ire	ier	
bird	fire	drier	

bird	fire	drier

r-Influenced Vowel Patterns or, ore, oar

soar	work	horse	more	store
sore	worse	roar	for	wore
four	floor	tore	storm	boar
corn	world	worm	hoarse	fork
			oar	poor

or	ore	oar	w+or	
form	shore	board	word	

Write on the lines words with the same vowel sound and pattern as form, shore, board, and word.

form	shore	board	word

nurse	purse	lure
injure	churn	nature
curb	cure	pure
surf	purple	future
splurge	burn	curse
hurt		

ur	ure	ur_e
turn	**sure**	**curve**

turn

sure

curve

torn	hard	score
earn	snore	nerve
snort	worth	card
bore	yard	spur
horse	search	jar
chore	bar	sharp
pearl	march	worst

ar	ər	or

| hard | score | earn | snore | nerve | pearl | worth | card | bore |
| yard | spur | horse | search | jar | chore | bar | sharp | torn |

ar

er

or

joy	soil	soy	join
ploy	moist	decoy	coin
boil	coy	coil	annoy
spoil	enjoy	broil	Roy
foil	oil	toy	Troy

oy
boy

oi
point

p	s	b	c	j	t	n	l	pl	nt

oi	oy

Sort 28: Diphthongs oi, oy

would	spoon	nook	fool
stool	could	hook	brook
crook	troop	root	hood
spool	wood	hoop	noon
groom	foot	tool	should
	soot	wool	stood

$\bar{oo} = \bar{u}$

soon

$\breve{oo}$

good

c f h st r l n k d t p

$\overline{oo} = \overline{u}$

$\overset{\smile}{oo}$

Vowel Digraphs aw, au

sauce	straw	taught	raw
fault	yawn	vault	paw
pause	crawl	maul	draw
law	haul	hawk	laugh
lawn	haunt	claw	cause
			launch

au					
caught					

aw					
saw					

s p l c d r h m e t v f n g y

aw	au

ground	south	mouth	pound
couch	frown	town	clown
drown	owl	howl	tough
plow	shout	growl	count
gown	scout	cloud	crown
	rough	found	grown

	OW				
	brown				

ou					
sound					

t h n l s d c b r f sc d g p

ou	ow

known	knit	rap
wreck	wreath	wren
wrist	knot	gnaw
knight	wrinkle	knob
wring	knee	ring
knead	gnash	wrap

gn								
gnat								

wr								
wrong								

kn								
knife								

Draw two pictures of things that begin with kn, wr, and gn. Write the word below each picture.

kn	wr	gn
_____	_____	_____
_____	_____	_____

Sort 32: Silent Beginning Consonants kn, wr, gn

stress	scrap	strict
straight	scream	string
scrape	spray	spruce
strange	squirrel	stripe
stretch	sprout	scram
scribe	spread	script
scratch		

Triple r-blends scr, str, spr

scr	str	spr	
screen	strong	spring	

scr	str	spr

throne	squirm	threw
shrink	shrub	shrug
squint	shriek	squeak
squeeze	threat	squish
squash	shrunk	throw
shrewd	thrill	shrimp
through	squawk	thrifty

squ							
square							

shr							
shred							

thr							
three							

thr	shr	squ

gentle	cub	gym	coat
cent	circle	gem	center
game	carrot	guide	guess
giraffe	cart	cell	guest
cycle	gist	golf	circus
ginger	calf	code	goose

hard g	soft g	hard c	soft c
gave	giant	card	city

Sort 35: Hard and Soft c and g   (141)

Say each word. Write on the lines words from the box that have each c or g sound.

cell goose gist coat calf gym cub cycle guest cart
golf code gem circle game circus ginger cent guide gentle

hard c	soft c	hard g	soft g

twelve	sense	glance
leave	prove	prince
glove	choose	wise
piece	cheese	bounce
solve	tease	love
peace	loose	shove
dance	those	since

-ce	-ve	-se
chance	move	please

Choose beginning and middle letters to make words with ending consonants -ce, -ve, and -se. Write each word on a line.

sh ch th pr d p b gl l s t n pl o an in en ea oo ee ie ou

-ce	-ve	-se

Name each picture. Circle the vowel sound you hear in the name.

1.	2.	3.	4.
ĕ ă ā	ō ū ŏ	ŏ ā ĭ	ŏ ŭ ē

5.	6.	7.	8.
ā ē ī	ū ō ŭ	ā ŏ ă	ă ĭ ĕ

9.	10.	11.	12.
ă ā ī	ĭ ĕ ū	ā ĕ ē	ŭ ū ĕ

13.	14.	15.	16.
ū ă ŭ	ĕ ĭ ē	ă ŭ ĕ	ū ō ē

17.	18.	19.	20.
ē ĭ ī	ī ē ā	ĕ ŏ ō	ē ā ă

Spell Check 1: Long and Short Vowel Sounds   147

Name each picture. Then write the name of the picture on the lines.

1.	2.	3.
_____	_____	_____
4.	5.	6.
_____	_____	_____
7.	8.	9.
_____	_____	_____
10.	11.	12.
_____	_____	_____
13.	14.	15.
_____	_____	_____

SPELL CHECK 3

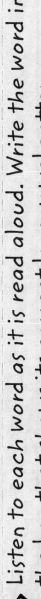

Listen to each word as it is read aloud. Write the word in the box that shows its correct long vowel pattern.

CV or CVV Open Syllable	CVVC	CVCe	CVCC

Name each picture. Then circle the correct spelling of the name.

SPELL CHECK 4

1.	2.	3.
fir fist **first**	corne corn coar	shirt shert shurt
4.	5.	6.
jar jare jaw	tier tire tyre	fare fair fear
7.	8.	9.
deer dear dere	warm worm wurm	fore four for
10.	11.	12.
chair chayre chare	star stare stair	hoarse house horse
13.	14.	15.
threat three thair	purse perse pirse	fourk furk fork

Spell Check 4: r-Influenced Vowel Patterns

Listen to each word as it is read aloud. Write the word in the box that shows its correct vowel pattern.

SPELL CHECK 5

aw	au	ow
_____	_____	_____
_____	_____	_____
_____	_____	_____
_____	_____	_____

ou	oy	oi
_____	_____	_____
_____	_____	_____
_____	_____	_____

Listen to each word as it is read aloud. Write the word in the box that shows its correct beginning consonant pattern.

squ	thr	shr
_____	_____	_____
_____	_____	_____
_____	_____	_____

scr	spr	str
_____	_____	_____
_____	_____	_____
_____	_____	_____

Spell Check 6: Beginning Complex Consonant Clusters

Listen to each word as it is read aloud. Write the word in the box that shows its correct beginning sound or word ending.

SPELL CHECK 6b

hard c or g	soft c or g	-ce
_____	_____	_____
_____	_____	_____
_____	_____	_____
_____	_____	_____

-se	-ve
_____	_____
_____	_____
_____	_____

Spell Check 6: Hard and Soft c and g and Word Endings -ce, -se, -ve